# Imitation in Early Christianity and Today

**Cornelis Bennema**
London School of Theology

GROVE BOOKS LIMITED
RIDLEY HALL RD CAMBRIDGE CB3 9HU

# Contents





**First Impression** March 2025
**ISSN** 1365-490X
**ISBN** 978 1 78827 451 7

# 1 Imitation and Christianity

Imitation (or mimesis) is central to human life. We are social beings and wired to imitate: babies learn to talk by imitating their parents; children grow up imitating their parents, teachers and other role models; adults progress in their behaviour and skills by imitating others. But people are not always aware or careful about what or whom they imitate. In popular culture, many people find their role models on social media, where influencers cultivate an often-uncritical following. Many people seem naive about whom they follow on social media or choose as examples. As a result, they are insufficiently aware about what or who influences their behaviour. Imitation can also take negative forms, so we tend to reject forms of imitation such as counterfeit goods, forged documents or plagiarized research. Our focus, however, is on how Christians can use imitation positively in discipleship.

In Christianity, imitation is an important ethical concept but has not received much attention. We will explore what history and the Bible can teach us about imitation and how to live well. While some forms of imitation happen unconsciously (see the example of infants, above), Christianity focuses on the conscious imitation of an exemplar (especially Jesus) in order to become like that person. Imitation is a means to moral development in that the goal of imitating Jesus is for a person to become Christlike. We will learn that authentic imitation is not about simplistic replication or cloning but a complex, creative process where the imitator observes the exemplar, discerns what is worthy of imitation, and then determines the shape of the imitative act.[1]

**Those who belong to Christ imitate him in order to become Christlike**

During the 1990s and early 2000s, the acronym WWJD (What Would Jesus Do) became popular among evangelical Christians, an expression of their desire to behave like Jesus, that is to imitate him. But often there were no guidelines as to what people could imitate about Jesus. Other sections of the church, however, such as the Reformed tradition, are critical of the concept of imitating Jesus because they consider such practice an infringement on the uniqueness of Christ. But the imitation and uniqueness of Christ need not be conflicting ideas because the call to imitate Christ is for those who are 'in Christ,' to use a Pauline phrase. In other words, people do not imitate Christ in order to become Christians; rather, those who already belong to Christ are called to imitate him in order to become Christlike. Hence, imitation is a subset of participation in Christ and the Christian moral life.

A quick glance at early Christian literature shows that the idea of imitation is prominent in John, Paul and the Apostolic Fathers, but rarely features in the rest of the New Testament. The term 'to imitate' (and its cognates) occurs eleven times in the New Testament (mainly in Paul) and eighteen times in the Apostolic Fathers.[2] In the Pauline tradition, we notice that Paul often issues the directive to imitate him (1 Cor 4.16; 11.1; Phil 3.17; 2 Thess 3.7, 9). Even though 1 Cor 11.1 clarifies that the call to imitate Paul is rooted in his imitation of Christ, it is nevertheless audacious. In addition, Paul wrote letters to churches when he was unable to be with them, so how could Pauline Christians imitate an absent Paul whom they could not observe? This seems to imply that imitation can happen through other means than direct observation.

In the Johannine tradition, the term 'to imitate' occurs only once (in 3 John 11) and John seems to prefer other language to express the idea of imitation. Imitation assumes a resemblance between the person who sets an example and the one who emulates it, so we could explore so-called comparative language—words such as 'like(wise),' '(just) as' and 'similarly.' Indeed, in the Johannine writings, we find the recurrent expression 'just as Jesus did, so also the disciples should do' (*eg* John 13.15, 34; 15.10; 17.14, 18, 21–22; 20.21; 1 John 2.6).

It is far more difficult to find a concept of imitation in the Synoptic gospels. While the literal terms for imitation do not occur in the Synoptics, some people assume that 'following Jesus' means imitating him. After all, should the disciples, besides taking in Jesus' teaching, not also learn by observing and imitating him? However, 'to follow' also has connotations of allegiance and obedience. Hence, rather than claiming that 'to follow' means 'to imitate,' it seems more accurate to say that following Jesus can *facilitate* the imitation of Jesus. Elsewhere, Matt 5.48 ('Be perfect...as your heavenly Father is perfect') and Luke 6.36 ('Be merciful, just as your Father is merciful') indicate imitation but the imitation of God is unusual and not explained.

Beyond the New Testament, the Apostolic Fathers in the first half of the second century present the new idea of martyrdom as the ideal imitation of Christ. For example, the martyrdom of Polycarp, Bishop of Smyrna, around AD 155, was presented as something all faithful Christians wished to imitate (Mart Pol 19.1). We will explore how the New Testament prepares for this extreme form of imitation. Before we do so, we should note that the idea of imitating an exemplary person did not originate in early Christianity but was common in Graeco-Roman antiquity and to a lesser extent in Jewish antiquity. Early Christian churches emerged across the Graeco-Roman world and were to an extent influenced by it, so we now turn to this period.

# Imitation in Graeco-Roman Antiquity

2

In Graeco-Roman antiquity, imitation originally referred to the representation of nature through the fine arts (dance, painting, sculpture, poetry), but over time it spread to the realms of religion, family and education to express the imitation of god, parent and teacher.[3] It is important to note that for the ancient Greeks and Romans, imitation was not so much about complete likeness or exact reproduction but more about creative, corresponding representation.[4] The broader context of imitation was Graeco-Roman society, where the primary concern was how to live well as a citizen. In the Greek city-state or *polis* and Roman society, the basic social unit was the family or household. Since the family functioned as a microcosm of the *polis*, the spheres of family and civic education often overlapped. Imitation became a crucial mechanism in moral and civic education where the imitation of suitable exemplars, especially from one's family, aided people in how to live well in the Greek *polis* or Roman society. We will explore this idea of imitation from classical Greek drama to the Graeco-Roman rhetorical traditions.

## Ancient Greek Theatre

In Greek antiquity, philosophy, theatre, poetry, music and the other arts were inextricably linked to daily life. Martha Nussbaum explains that at religious festivals (especially in honour of Dionysos), the entire city gathered to watch and rate the performance of several dramas. Dramas in ancient Greek theatre were assessed on their ethical and political content, and the spectators were actively involved in deliberation through strong emotional responses.[5] As Ferenc Hörcher states, Greek drama imitated or represented contemporaneous events with actors personifying protagonists as they played out the story in front of an audience that responded emotionally and intellectually. Hence, through the medium of drama and its inbuilt element of imitation, Athenian citizens learnt about civic life: how to behave as virtuous citizens and what mistakes to avoid.[6] Classical Athenian drama, therefore, was not only about entertainment but was used in service of moral and civic education. We now turn to the Graeco-Roman rhetorical traditions because their moral discourses are instructive about how imitation worked. We will start with Isocrates, a prominent orator and educator in classical Athens. Isocrates was an example for Cicero, who in turn influenced Seneca and Quintilian, so we can expect a degree of continuity in their understanding of imitation.

## Graeco-Roman Rhetorical Traditions

Greek orator Isocrates (436–338 BCE) was the first to employ imitation as a method for moral education.[7] In his famous discourse *Evagoras*, Isocrates presents the late king Evagoras as a model ruler to Evagoras's son Nicocles for contemplation, study and imitation in order to achieve moral progress: 'For we exhort young men to the study of philosophy by praising others in order that they, emulating those who are eulogized, may desire to adopt the same pursuits, but I appeal to you and yours, using as examples not aliens, but members of your own family…[I]f you persevere in the study of philosophy and make as great progress as heretofore, you will soon become the man it is fitting you should be' (*Evagoras* 77, 81).[8]

Cicero (106–43 BCE) was a Roman orator, philosopher and statesman, and the theme of imitation occurs frequently in *De Officiis*, a three-volume treatise to instruct his son Marcus. Cicero's advice to those who aspire to greatness in public life is to select suitable examples for imitation and to associate with them in order to become like them. Here is an excerpt: 'Young men win recognition most easily and most favourably, if they attach themselves to men who are at once wise and renowned as well as patriotic counsellors in public affairs. And if they associate constantly with such men, they inspire in the public the expectation that they will be like them, seeing that they have themselves selected them for imitation' (*Off* 2.46). Cicero indicates that discernment is essential to the process of imitation. He warns against blindly imitating everything about one's ancestors; one should not imitate their faults nor those virtues that are beyond one's abilities (*Off* 1.121).

**Cicero's advice is to select suitable examples for imitation and to associate with them**

Seneca (4 BCE–65 CE) was a Stoic philosopher and statesman. In his collection of moral letters to Lucilius, the procurator of Sicily during Nero's reign, Seneca urges him to associate with appropriate role models: 'Cleanthes could not have been the express image of Zeno, if he had merely heard his lectures; he shared in his life, saw into his hidden purposes, and watched him to see whether he lived according to his own rules. Plato, Aristotle, and the whole throng of sages who were destined to go each his different way, derived more benefit from the character than from the words of Socrates. It was not the classroom of Epicurus, but living together under the same roof, that made great men of Metrodorus, Hermarchus, and Polyaenus' (*Epistle* 6.6). While Seneca acknowledges the value of historic examples, he recommends living examples because their lives can be readily observed.

Quintilian (35–100 CE), an educator and orator, produced the *Institutio Oratoria*, a twelve-volume textbook on the theory and practice of rhetoric. Like Seneca, he notes that personal example is crucial in education and much more powerful than just instruction: 'For in everything which we teach, examples are more effective even than the rules which are taught in the schools...And the reason is this, that the professor of rhetoric lays down rules, while the orator gives a practical demonstration' (*Inst* 10.1.15). Quintilian stresses the need for discernment and improvement in education: 'First we must consider whom to imitate. For there are many who have shown a passionate desire to imitate the worst and most decadent authors. Secondly, we must consider what it is that we should set ourselves to imitate in the authors thus chosen' (*Inst* 10.2.14).

## A Graeco-Roman Model of Imitation

Our examination shows that imitation was an important educational strategy for moral and civic education—from ancient Athenian drama where its audience learnt how to live as good citizens, to the writings of Graeco-Roman orators who saw example and imitation as key to good citizenship. Young people were encouraged to select good role models and discern what aspects to imitate, so imitation was seen as instrumental in shaping young people's character and conduct, enabling them to live well in society.

Based on our findings, we can construct a common model of the workings of imitation in Graeco-Roman antiquity comprising five aspects:

- *Selection and association*. Aspiring students choose or are presented with an exemplary person for imitation and associate themselves with that person.
- *Observation*. Imitation is by nature a sensory process where one must closely observe exemplary people in order to imitate them.
- *Discernment*. In studying the exemplar, the imitator must discern what is worthy of imitation. Hence, imitation should not be reduced to a mechanical process of simplistic repetition.
- *Imitation*. Having observed and understood the model, the imitator articulates this in a concrete imitative act that shows correspondence with the original example.
- *Transformation*. Insofar as imitation relates to education or family, the aim is moral development where one imitates the teacher or parent in order to become a better person.

Before we move to the early Christian writings, we must consider the authoritative source document for early Christians—the Old Testament—and later Jewish writings around the time of the New Testament.

# 3 Imitation in Jewish Antiquity

In the Old Testament there are traces of imitation but the idea is not developed. We can think of texts such as Gen 1.26, where humankind is created in the image of God (but this refers more to representation); Lev 19.2, where God commands the Israelites to be holy because he is holy (but the connection is causal rather than comparative); and Deut 10.18–19, saying that God looks after the outsider and that the Israelites should also love the outsider because they were once outsiders in Egypt (but this may simply denote analogy). More generally, Israel is often urged 'to walk in the way of the Lord' and 'to follow after God,' but this seems to refer more to obedience and allegiance than imitation. Nevertheless, while the idea of imitating God may not be explicit, the Old Testament does not simply present God as the lawgiver and source of ethical commands; it also portrays him as the paradigm of moral behaviour in that Israelites are encouraged to model their behaviour on God's.[9]

**The Old Testament presents godly people as implicit examples for imitation**

In addition to the implied imitation of God, the Old Testament also presents godly people or behaviour as implicit examples for imitation. The stories of virtuous Old Testament figures, such as Abraham, Moses, Ruth, David and Esther, serve as examples for imitation, although the authors do not specify what aspects of these exemplars readers are to imitate. Old Testament wisdom literature (Proverbs, Psalms, Ecclesiastes) illustrates good and bad examples for imitation. Turning to the prophets, the Book of Amos is an indictment of Israel's failure to ensure social justice, which God not only demands but has exemplified in Israel's history. Or consider the Book of Jonah, revealing that Jonah (and Israel) failed to imitate God's compassion and mercy. In sum, while it would be presumptuous to claim that the Old Testament promotes the idea of imitation, it nevertheless contains the *seeds* of imitation.

When Greek culture starts to influence Jewish thought (a process called Hellenization), we see these seeds come to fruition in several Jewish writings of the Second Temple period. A few examples will help. In Wis Sol 4.2, the author notes that when virtue is present or available, people imitate it. In 4 Macc 13.9, when certain Jews are tortured by Greek king Antiochus IV, they take Shadrach, Meshach and Abednego as models for imitation to remain faithful (see Dan 3.12). Jewish historian Josephus uses the concept of imitation when recounting Old Testament leaders for his readers. He notes, for example, that early in his reign Solomon imitated David but later he started to imitate the practices of his foreign wives (*Ant* 8.24, 193). When Jewish philosopher Philo speaks of humans as an imitation and representation of God (*Opif* 139; *Det* 83), he takes the implied idea of imitation in Gen 1.26–27 and makes it explicit. Finally, the Jewish rabbis were conscious that their lives were visible examples for their pupils to imitate.[10] The well-known anecdote of Rabbi Kahana, who hid underneath the bed of his teacher when he and his wife had sexual intercourse, shows how far the idea of observing the teacher could go (b *Ber* 62a). When we come to early Christianity, the Graeco-Roman concept of imitation had also found its way into the New Testament (especially John and Paul) and the Apostolic Fathers.

# 4 Imitation in John

The literal term for imitation occurs only once in the Johannine tradition—in 3 John 11, as a general command to imitate what is good and not what is evil. John, however, uses comparative language to express the concept of imitation. The most frequent Johannine construction that indicates imitation is this: 'Just as [Jesus] did, [the disciples] also should do.' Jesus often sets the example of ethical living for the disciples to imitate. The passage that shows this best is the foot washing in John 13.

## The Foot Washing and a Johannine Model of Imitation

John 13.1–17 is ideal for understanding imitation in John because it contains Jesus' first explicit imitative imperative to the disciples (John 13.15), and the story in which this imperative is embedded (John 13.1–17) describes the various workings of imitation. The foot washing pericope has two sections, each expressing a different but related meaning: in John 13.1–11 Jesus alludes to the disciples' (spiritual) purification that he will finalize for them on the cross, while in John 13.12–17 Jesus explains the foot washing as humble, loving service that needs regular repetition. I will concentrate on John 13.4–5, 12–17, the important part for the notion of imitation. John 13.4–5 and 12a bookend the physical act of foot washing. Three consecutive verbs describe Jesus' actions at the start (he stands up from the table, removes his garment and washes his disciples' feet) and in reverse order at the end (having washed his disciples' feet, he puts on his garment and reclines again at the table). Usually, one can only imitate what one observes. Indeed, instead of *telling* the disciples that they should wash one another's feet, Jesus *shows* what needs imitation. Only then does Jesus issue the command to imitate him, 'For I gave you an example, that just as I did to you, you also should do' (John 13.15). The example that he refers to, of course, is the foot washing—the visible model for imitation.

We must now consider whether the command in John 13.15 calls for a literal replication of the foot washing or is a broad call to humble, loving service. An important clue is to note that authentic imitation requires *understanding*. When Jesus goes back to the table after the foot washing he does not immediately tell the disciples to imitate his example. Instead, he asks in John 13.12b, 'Do you know (*ie* understand) what I have done to you?' Jesus checks whether the disciples have understood what he did for them, so they must *interpret*

Jesus' example in order to imitate him. This implies that imitation cannot be a mindless cloning or simplistic replication. Instead, imitation requires two stages—the understanding of the original example and the resulting imitative act. It follows that, for John, imitation is a cognitive process where the believer has to interpret Jesus' example in order to imitate it. I call this 'moral reasoning,' that is, thinking in line with God's character, values and norms, as exemplified by Jesus. Consequently, the imitator must understand the intent of the original act and articulate this understanding in a corresponding imitative act. While this does not rule out the literal practice of foot washing as an expression of humble, loving service, it does not exhaust the scope of what Jesus meant. The intention behind Jesus' actions here is that the disciples understand the need for humble, loving service to one another *and* produce a concrete act that faithfully expresses this understanding.

**Imitation relates to both behaviour and identity**

In John 13.13–14, 16, Jesus gives the rationale for the command in John 13.15. An argument from the greater to the lesser clarifies why the disciples are not excused from imitating Jesus: what the one of higher status (Jesus) has done, those of lower status (disciples) must also do. In addition, Jesus, the Lord and teacher, identifies and acts as a slave, so the disciples' imitation cannot simply be the performance of an act of service but must involve participation in Jesus' slave-identity and becoming slaves to one another. Hence, imitation relates to both behaviour and identity. Jesus then says, 'If you understand these things, you are blessed if you do them' (John 13.17), where the term 'blessed' or 'happy' refers to God's favour bestowed on the imitator. But in what way? I suggest that in adopting a servant attitude and performing acts of humble, loving service in imitation of Jesus, the imitator will gradually become more like Jesus.

We can now see the contours of a Johannine model of imitation that is similar to that in Graeco-Roman antiquity: (1) observation (John 13.4–5, 12a); (2) discernment (John 13.12b); (3) imitation (John 13.14–15); (4) transformation (John 13.17). To complete the model, we can add a first stage 'selection and association' from the Johannine writings, where Jesus chooses his disciples and invites them to associate with him (John 1.39; 6.70; 15.16) and, at another level, John encourages his audience to select and associate ('remain') with Jesus (John 6.35–40, 60–71; 15.1–7; 20.31).

## Other Instances of Imitation in John

In John 13.34, Jesus states the famous love command: 'I give you a new commandment, that you love one another. Just as I have loved you, you also should love one another' (see also John 15.12). While the first part of John 13.34 states the love command, the second half explains it as a command of imitation. The significance is that the love command is not given in a vacuum but proceeds from a precedent. In other words, the disciples' love for one another is based on their personal experience of Jesus' love for them—as they have, for example, experienced in the foot washing (see also John 13.1). This means that Jesus' love for the disciples is the empowering model for their love for one another. Imitation thus springs from a relationship with Jesus where believers have observed and experienced Jesus' love for themselves, which in turn, empowers them to love others. How imitating Jesus' love in their love for one another will look in different situations requires moral reasoning, just as we saw in the footwashing.

While the foot washing and the love command are the most obvious instances of Johannine imitation, John's characteristic imitative language, 'just as [Jesus] did, [the disciples] also should do,' applies to other areas of the believer-Jesus imitation:

- *Obedience*: just as Jesus has kept his Father's commandments and (hence) abides in his love, so the disciples should imitate Jesus (John 15.10). Jesus' obedience to the Father (and his consequent abiding in the Father's love) is the example for the disciples to imitate, so they should obey Jesus and continue to abide in his love.
- *Unity*: 'As you, Father, are in me and I am in you, may they also be in us...' and 'so that they may be one, as we are one' (John 17.21–22; 17.11). While the previous examples show how believers imitate Jesus through actions, this example refers to what I call imitating a state of being or existential imitation where the indwelling of believers by the Father and Son is patterned on and an extension of the intimate relationship between the Father and Son. For John, this reality is not static or passive but refers to a dynamic and transformative relationship, which affects both the believers' identity and behaviour.
- *Existence*: in John 17.14, 16, Jesus states that just as he does not belong to the world, so the disciples do not belong to the world, that is, they no longer have their origins in this world. Any person, by physical birth, belongs to the natural world or realm below, but a birth of God or the Spirit brings them into the world of God or realm above (John 1.13; 3.5). Consequently, believers imitate or mirror Jesus' existence, so they are no longer of the world because they have become of God.
- *Mission*: 'As the Father has sent me, so I send you' (John 20.21; cf John 17.18). These verses express a twofold imitation. First, Jesus

imitates the Father in sending others into the world. But there is also an implied existential imitation in that the disciples' state of being sent into the world by Jesus imitates Jesus' state of being sent into the world by God. Hence, the disciples actively participate in the Father's mission through imitation.

It appears that a pattern emerges where Jesus regularly sets the example that the disciples can then, and therefore, imitate. It must be noted that Jesus' method of *teaching by example* originated from his Father. In John 5.19–20, Jesus says that he does nothing by himself but only what he sees the Father do. Other passages mention specific activities where Jesus imitates the Father, such as to give life (John 5.21, 26), speak (John 12.49–50; see also John 8.26; 15.15), love (John 15.9) and send (John 17.18; 20.21). The point is that the Son does not act independently or on his own initiative; rather, the Father provides the example for the Son to follow. Hence, the Son carries out the Father's work on earth *through imitation*, thus being the visible and audible manifestation of the Father. In imitating the Father, the Son unveils the heavenly realm and reveals the Father so people can observe and experience God for themselves (John 1.18, 51; 14.9). Jesus thus represents on earth the invisible God by means of imitation. There is a chain of imitation, where the Father sets the example for the Son, and the Son sets the example for his followers.

Turning to 1 John, we learn that John applies moral reasoning and develops *new* forms of imitation from Jesus' personal example and teaching. Here are some examples:

- 1 John 2.6: Just as [Jesus] walked, the one who claims to abide in him must also walk (likewise). 'To walk' is shorthand for 'way of life,' referring to Jesus' life on earth as a model for imitation. John may have derived this command from Jesus' saying in John 14.6 that he is the 'way' of life in which people should walk. How this might look in various situations will, of course, require moral reasoning.
- 1 John 3.3: 'All who have this hope in him purify themselves, just as he [Jesus] is pure.' This call to imitation is perhaps rooted in John 17.19. Although the idea of imitation is weak—it does not say that believers must purify themselves just as Jesus purified himself (because Jesus is pure)—it nevertheless urges believers to imitate Jesus' purity.
- 1 John 3.7: 'The one who does what is right is righteous, just as he is righteous.' This example of imitation may be influenced by John 5.30 and John 7.24.

- 1 John 3.16: 'We know love by this, that he laid down his life for us—and we ought to lay down our lives for one another.' John does not simply remind his audience of Jesus' saying in John 15.13 but turns it into a new form of imitation: just as Jesus laid down his life for the sake of his followers, so they should lay down their lives for each other. John's subsequent progression from imitating Jesus' sacrificial love in 1 John 3.16 to the concrete imitative act of giving economic help to a fellow believer in 1 John 3.17 clearly displays moral reasoning.
- 1 John 4.11: 'Since God loved us so much, we also ought to love one another.' This imitative command is a conflation of John 3.16 and John 13.34.

Our examination shows that Johannine ethics is primarily *imitation ethics*, that is, imitation is central to John's ethical thought. Believers imitate Jesus in serving one another, loving one another, being united with one another and so on, so that they may *become* people characterized by service, love and unity—in short, to become more like Jesus. We now turn to the other main imitation theologian in the New Testament—the apostle Paul.

# 5

# Imitation in Paul

The Pauline corpus contains eight of the eleven occurrences of the term 'to imitate' (and its cognates) in the New Testament (1 Thess 1.6; 2.14; 2 Thess 3.7, 9; 1 Cor 4.16; 11.1; Phil 3.17; Eph 5.1). Five of these mention Paul's call to imitate him (2 Thess 3.7, 9; 1 Cor 4.16; 11.1; Phil 3.17; but see also 1 Thess 1.6; Gal 4.12), although Christ remains the ultimate object of imitation (1 Cor 11.1). We will focus on the Thessalonian, Corinthian and Philippian correspondence, which not only contains the majority of references to imitation but also reflects the early, middle and later period of Paul's ministry. We will then briefly search for possible ideas of imitation in the remaining Pauline letters to get a complete picture.

## 1–2 Thessalonians

The Thessalonian correspondence contains half of the Pauline references to imitation (1 Thess 1.6; 2.14; 2 Thess 3.7, 9) and a quarter of the instances of the term 'example' (1 Thess 1.7; 2 Thess 3.9), so these early letters are instructive for understanding the concept of imitation in Pauline thought. Paul's chief concern is to instruct the Thessalonians on how to live in a manner worthy of God (1 Thess 2.12), in view of persecution and the parousia (1 Thess 1.9–10; 3.13; 4.1), and his strategy involves the use of example and imitation.

In 1 Thess 1.6 we read that the Thessalonians had become imitators of Paul but it is not clear whether it is their steadfast and joyful endurance of suffering on account of their faith (1 Thess 1.6b) or their adoption of Paul's general lifestyle (1 Thess 1.5b) that made them imitators of Paul. I contend that 1 Thess 1.5b provides the example for imitation, whereas 1 Thess 1.6b mentions the starting point of imitation. I take 1 Thess 1.6b to mean that the Thessalonians became imitators of Paul (and his team) *after* they had accepted the word amidst persecution, and that in 1 Thess 1.5b Paul reminds the Thessalonians of the way he and his team lived for their sake. This suggests that the Thessalonians had been able to observe Paul and his team during their visit to Thessalonica (see also Acts 17.1–9). Although Paul does not provide details of his lifestyle in 1 Thess 1.5b, he does so in 1 Thess 2.1–12. The content of imitation mentioned in 1 Thess 1.6a, therefore, is not found in 1.6b but in 1 Thess 1.5b and is elaborated in 1 Thess 2.1–12 when Paul alludes to his past visit and the lifestyle he had modelled for them.

The Thessalonians not only imitated the example of Paul but, in turn, became an example for other believers throughout Macedonia and Achaia on living out the gospel amidst persecution (1 Thess 1.7). Hence, there is an imitative chain from Paul (and the Lord) to the Thessalonian Christians to other Christians across Greece. When we turn to 2 Thess 3.7–9, we learn that some Thessalonian Christians had failed to imitate a particular aspect of Paul's lived example, namely to work for a living and not to depend on others (see 1 Thess 2.9; 4.11). So, Paul urges those Thessalonians to imitate him and work for a living. Even from this brief survey we can see that imitation is vital to Paul's strategy for the moral formation of the Thessalonian church.

## 1 Corinthians

Twice in 1 Corinthians, Paul issues the injunction to imitate him (1 Cor 4.16; 11.1). We first turn to 1 Cor 4.16–17, where we find that the imitation of Paul is mediated through Timothy. The immediate context of 1 Cor 4.14–17 contains rich family language: (i) Paul describes himself as the (spiritual) father of the Corinthians (1 Cor 4.15); (ii) the Corinthians are Paul's beloved children (1 Cor 4.14); and (iii) Timothy is Paul's beloved and faithful child (1 Cor 4.17). Hence, Paul places the concept of imitation in the context of family education. In his absence, Paul is sending Timothy to help the Corinthian church in imitating him. Paul's assertion that Timothy will remind them of his 'ways in Christ Jesus' is probably shorthand for his way of life patterned after Christ's. While Paul's call to imitate him refers generally to the imitation of his overall lifestyle, 1 Cor 4.9–13 indicates that it refers specifically to his extreme self-abasement and self-giving as the antidote for the Corinthians' arrogance and boasting in leaders.[11] Paul would most likely not send Timothy to simply repeat verbally his teaching but also to exemplify the life he desires for the Corinthians, so that the Corinthians can imitate Paul by observing Timothy. Paul is the spiritual parent of both Timothy and the Corinthians, and by sending Timothy, Paul presents him as an exemplary child to help his other 'children' to imitate him.

**Paul places the concept of imitation in the context of family education**

The injunction to imitate Paul in 1 Cor 11.1, as part of the conclusion 1 Cor 10.31–11.1 to 1 Cor 8–10, is a general call not to use one's personal rights if that would lead other believers to sin. Paul's clarification 'just as I [imitate] Christ' indicates his awareness that he is merely a link in an imitative chain in which Christ is the main example for imitation. While there is debate about whether Paul referred to the imitation of the earthly Jesus or risen Christ, Victor Copan explains that ancient writers assumed that the readers were familiar with the story of a hero from the past, so that a simple reference to imitate such a person would be sufficient to recall the relevant tradition surrounding the exemplar. Hence, when Paul refers to his imitation of Christ, he assumes that the Corinthians would draw on the proper parallels in the Jesus tradition that correspond to Paul's example to inform their imitation.[12] The imitation of Christ is mediated through Paul *not* because Paul had seen the Lord and the Corinthians had not, nor because the Corinthians did not know about the earthly Jesus, but because the Corinthians were immature and needed to learn to imitate Christ through Paul.

## Philippians

Paul's ambition for the Philippian Christians was to present them as 'blameless' at the parousia (Phil 1.10), and he states the central case of this letter in Phil 1.27, 'Live your life in a manner worthy of the gospel of Christ.' His strategy for promoting a gospel lifestyle among the Philippian Christians involves imitation. Paul first presents Christ as the supreme example for imitation in the familiar passage Phil 2.5–11 (see *eg* the ideas of humility in Phil 2.3, 8 and obedience in Phil 2.8, 12), but he also presents himself and others as models for imitation.

In introducing himself as 'a slave of Christ' in Phil 1.1, Paul likens his position to the slave-status of Christ in Phil 2.7 (the Greek *doulos* only occurs in 1.1 and 2.7 in the letter), showing the Philippians that he is an imitator of Christ. In Phil 1.20–25, Paul ponders the outcome of his imminent trial in Rome. Oscillating between life and death, Paul ultimately desires *not* what is best for him but what is best for the Philippian church. Paul's attitude exemplifies what he goes on to urge the Philippians to do in Phil 2.4, namely to imitate the attitude of Christ in Phil 2.6–8 that prioritizes the interest of others. Then, in Phil 2.17, Paul declares his willingness to pour out his life for the sake of the Philippians, demonstrating that he imitates Christ pouring out his life for the sake of humanity in Phil 2.7. In Phil 3.17a, Paul urges the Philippians to join with one another in imitating him. While Christ remains the supreme example for imitation, the Philippians can imitate Christ by imitating Paul (see also 1 Cor 11.1). Consequently, in Phil 4.9, Paul urges the Philippians to keep on doing, that is imitating, what that they had observed him do when he was with them.

**Paul holds up Timothy and Epaphroditus as examples for imitation because they imitate aspects of Christ**

Besides himself, Paul holds up Timothy and Epaphroditus as examples for imitation because they imitate aspects of Christ. Timothy's description as 'slave' in Phil 1.1 and 'to serve as a slave' in Phil 2.22 echoes Christ's slave status in Phil 2.7, while the mention of his genuine concern for the Philippians in Phil 2.20 reflects the ideal of Phil 2.4 and imitates Christ's selfless interest in others. Regarding

Epaphroditus, the recurrent phrase 'to the point of death' in Phil 2.8 and Phil 2.30 indicates that his near-death experience for the sake of Christ has echoes of Christ's death for the sake of humanity. In Phil 3.17b, Paul even points the Philippians to other Christians living in line with his lifestyle and providing a visible example for imitation in Paul's absence. So, Paul uses the concepts of example and imitation as a moral strategy for promoting 'blameless' Christian living (Phil 2.15) in the Philippian church.

## Other Pauline Letters

The idea of personal example and imitation can also be found in other Pauline letters, albeit less prominent than those presented above. There is no explicit imitative language in Galatians, but scholars have noted an implied imitation in Gal 4.12, where Paul urges the Galatians, 'Become like me, for I also have become like you.' Noting the familial language in Gal 4.19 ('my little children'), de Boer, for example, states that 'The Galatians are being called by their father to be real children of his, and to show this by their likeness to him.'[13] In Romans, the clearest case of imitation is found in Rom 15.7, 'Therefore, accept one another, just as Christ also has accepted you.' We should probably understand this injunction in light of Rom 15.1–3, so that Paul specifically exhorts the 'strong' Roman believers to accept the 'weak' in imitation of Christ accepting them.[14]

A significant part of Paul's ministry was dedicated to collecting money from the churches in Macedonia and Achaia to assist the impoverished Jerusalem church (Rom 15.25–27). The Corinthian church in Achaia was keen to participate in Paul's project but apparently slow to act (2 Cor 8.10–11), so to help them act on their promise, Paul exhorts them to imitate the Macedonian churches, which had given generously despite their poverty and the persecution they faced (2 Cor 8.1–4). In Ephesians, the only explicit reference to imitation is found in Eph 5.1, the injunction to be imitators of God. This is the only place in the Pauline corpus where believers are commanded to imitate God (but see also Col 3.13). The immediate context of Eph 4.32–5.2 shows that Paul exhorts believers to imitate God in sacrificial love and forgiveness.

In the Pastoral Epistles, Paul presents Timothy and Titus as examples for imitation. In his absence, Paul commands Timothy to be a trustworthy example for the Ephesian believers in speech, conduct, love, faith and purity (1 Tim 4.12). As one of Paul's most trusted coworkers, Timothy has been a frequent example for imitation to Christians in Thessalonica, Corinth and Philippi (see above). While Timothy remained in Ephesus, Paul left Titus in Crete to look after the church there (Titus 1.5). In Titus 2.6-8, Paul commands Titus to exhort the young men to be of sound mind in two ways: (i) in conduct, by showing himself to be an example of good works; (ii) in teaching, by showing integrity, seriousness and speech beyond reproach. Hence, Paul charges Titus to show exemplary behaviour to the Cretan Christians.

## A Pauline Model of Imitation

Paul had to develop extensive ethics for his churches since most of his converts came from pagan backgrounds and were unfamiliar with Jewish-Christian values. Paul considers himself the spiritual father of those who became Christians through his ministry and calls them to imitate him, so they can reach maturity in Christ.[15] For Paul, imitation was a crucial mechanism for moral transformation and we can infer a model of imitation from his writings that resembles that in Graeco-Roman antiquity (and the Johannine writings):

- *Selection and association.* While Christ is the supreme example for imitation, Paul is often presented as an example for imitation, or in his absence, trusted coworkers such as Timothy, Epaphroditus and Titus, or even mature Christians.
- *Observation.* Sometimes Paul's converts are able to observe him, but in his absence they can observe others who exemplify Paul's lifestyle. Besides direct observation, Paul can present his audience with an example in his letters. In hearing the letter being read out, his audience can construct a mental picture of the example for imitation. Hence, Pauline Christians could observe exemplary models from embodied lives or written accounts.
- *Interpretation and imitation.* The model for imitation, whether Christ, Paul, Paul's trusted coworkers or other mature Christians, was not simply to be observed but also examined in order to avoid a reductionist concept of imitation. In 2 Thess 3.7–9, for example, the imperative to engage in physical labour to earn a living is not a command to do exactly the same work Paul did, but to engage, *like* Paul, in work to earn a living and not burden fellow believers by living off them.
- *Transformation.* We noted that the Pauline tradition presents Christ as the supreme example for moral transformation, and as the imitation of Christ is mediated through Paul and other examples, the goal is that believers become Christlike.

# 6 Imitation in the Apostolic Fathers

Beyond the New Testament, imitation also features in the Apostolic Fathers (see also note 2), where the idea of martyrdom as the ideal imitation of Christ emerged in the first half of the second century. We will examine the writings of Clement of Rome, Ignatius of Antioch and Polycarp of Smyrna and show that influences from both Johannine and Pauline traditions can explain the emergence of this new martyrological imitation.

## Clement of Rome

In 1 Clement, written to the church in Corinth at the end of the first century, Clement introduces examples for imitation from past and present to address the envy, strife and division that characterize the Corinthian church (see *eg* 1 Clem 3.1–4).[16] Having presented examples from Israel's past of those who were persecuted out of envy, such as Abel, Jacob, Joseph, Moses and David (1 Clem 4.1–13), Clement turns to the examples of Peter and Paul, who suffered martyrdom because of envy (1 Clem 5.1–7). In addition to the apostles, Clement speaks of a multitude of Christians who also suffered martyrdom because of envy and he presents them collectively as an excellent example to follow (1 Clem 6.1).

In 1 Clem 16.17, Clement first presents Christ's humility amidst suffering as an example to follow, and then exhorts the Corinthian Christians to be imitators of Israel's heroes who exemplified humility such as the prophets Elijah, Elisha and Ezekiel, as well as Abraham, Moses, Job and David (1 Clem 17.1–18.17). Having reminded the Corinthian church of these many great examples, Clement exhorts them to the practice of peace (*ie* harmony, unity) through the contemplation of God, literally, 'to gaze at God with the mind' (1 Clem 19.1–3). In keeping with the general principle of being able to observe the one whom one seeks to imitate, Clement urges the Corinthian Christians to look to God the creator as an example of good works (1 Clem 33.8).

In sum, Clement presents an array of past and present examples who have shown (i) steadfast endurance amidst persecution and martyrdom, (ii) humility and (iii) good works to counter a potential schism in the Corinthian church. James Petitfils notes that while Clement draws on Roman models of exemplary leadership, he preserves Pauline traditions in emphasizing the virtues of love and humility.[17] However, love and humility are also virtues to be imitated in the Johannine tradition, so it seems more accurate to say that Clement preserved a distinct *Christian* tradition of imitation.

## Ignatius of Antioch

In the letters of Ignatius, the bishop of Antioch, who was martyred in Rome in the early second century, several instances of imitation relate to unity—the dominant motif in the Ignatian corpus. In *Eph* 5.1, Ignatius's assertion that the church is united to Christ, as Christ is to God, hints at the idea of imitation in that the unity between Christ and the church is patterned on the unity between Christ and God. When Ignatius urges the Philadelphian Christians to be imitators of Christ, just as Christ is of God, he does so in a context of commending purity and unity (*Phld* 7.2). In *Magn* 7.1, Ignatius exhorts the Magnesian Christians to be obedient to the bishop, just as Christ (when he was on earth) was obedient to God, so that there may be unity. A similar idea is found in the exhortation that everyone should follow (*ie* obey) the bishop just as Christ followed the Father (*Smyrn* 8.1). The idea of achieving unity through imitation can be traced back to John 17 which mentions imitation in relation to unity.

Other Ignatian texts also contain imitative ideas that can be traced back to John. In *Eph* 6.1, the phrase 'to receive the bishop as we would receive Christ who sent him' echoes Jesus' saying in John 13.20. In *Magn* 7.1, the idea that the Magnesian Christians should not do anything without the permission of the bishop and elders, just as Jesus did nothing without the consent of the Father, is evidently derived from John 5.19. Nevertheless, the Ignatian corpus also shows Pauline influences. In *Phld* 11.1, Ignatius's gratitude that the Philadelphians have welcomed certain Christian workers just as Christ had also welcomed the Philadelphians, echoes the Pauline imitative imperative in Rom 15.7. In *Pol* 5.1, the exhortation to husbands to love their wives as Christ loves the church is derived from Eph 5.25.

Ignatius also holds up exemplary people for imitation. In *Eph* 1.3, he expresses his desire for the Ephesian Christians to imitate their exemplary bishop Onesimus. In *Smyrn* 12.1, Ignatius presents Burrhus as an exemplary minister of God whom everyone should imitate. In *Eph* 10.1–3, Ignatius encourages the Ephesian Christians to show exemplary behaviour to win over unbelievers to become disciples (*Eph* 10.1). As Candida Moss asserts, 'Learning to be a disciple from the deeds of the Christians involves imitation.'[18] In *Rom* 4.2 and 6.3, Ignatius expresses his desire to be a martyr in imitation of Christ. As Paul Hartog states, '[F]or Ignatius, imitation is the core of discipleship' and '[T]he ultimate manifestation of discipleship was martyrdom.'[19] So, for Ignatius, martyrdom is the supreme imitation of Christ and evidence of true discipleship.

## Polycarp of Smyrna

Polycarp's letter *To the Philippians* contains the idea of imitation. In *Phil* 1.1, Polycarp expresses his delight that the Philippian Christians have 'received the imitations of true love' and accompanied those who were bound in chains. If 'true love' is a reference to Christ, Polycarp may be referring to Ignatius and other prisoners as imitators of Christ in their sufferings (see also *Phil* 1.2, which mentions Christ's martyrdom).[20] In *Phil* 8–10, Polycarp mentions several examples for imitation. In *Phil* 8.2, he exhorts the Philippians to be(come) imitators of Christ's steadfast endurance amidst suffering because Christ himself has set this example. Then, in *Phil* 9.1, Polycarp urges them to practice the same endurance that they have observed in others, such as Ignatius, Zosimus, Rufus, Paul and other apostles.[21] Finally, in *Phil* 10.1, Polycarp urges the Philippians to follow the example of Christ in faithful endurance.

The anonymous letter Martyrdom of Polycarp describes the death of Polycarp in the mid-second century and presents martyrdom as the supreme imitation of Christ. From the outset, Polycarp is presented as an imitator of Christ in martyrdom in order to encourage other Christians also to imitate Christ in martyrdom (Mart Pol 1.2). In Mart Pol 17.3, the author explicitly declares that a martyr is a disciple and imitator of Christ, and in Mart Pol 19.1, Polycarp is depicted as a pre-eminent martyr, whom many desire to imitate in keeping with the gospel of Christ. In weaker form, the same idea is expressed in Mart Pol 22.1, that following the example of Polycarp will lead martyrs into the kingdom of Christ. As Moss explains, 'Polycarp is part of a mimetic chain, one that connects the audience of the martyrdom to Christ himself.'[22]

The Apostolic Fathers are significant for understanding early Christianity because they are the bridge between the apostles and the next generation of early Christian leadership, and it is during this time that the concept of martyrdom as the ideal imitation of Christ emerged. While we may ask whether such emphasis is mentally healthy, the idea of imitating Jesus' death can be traced back, for example, via John's newly-created imitative command in 1 John 3.16 to Jesus' own saying in John 15.13. At the same time, Moss helpfully asserts, '[T]he gospel-worthy martyr does not offer him- or herself for martyrdom but eagerly embraces it once the sentence is passed.'[23]

# 7

# Imitating Jesus Today

Our common model of imitation in Graeco-Roman antiquity and early Christianity is a good basis for considering how the imitation of Jesus can work today.

*Selection and association.* Imitation ethics is concerned with how abstract moral principles are lived out or embodied in the lives of exemplary people. In Christianity, Jesus is the supreme example for imitation, so when people become followers of Jesus, they should seek to model their lives on Jesus. The Bible is the main source of information about Jesus but there are other means to learn how to imitate Jesus. Just as Paul presents himself and others as examples for imitation to his new converts, so Christians who exemplify Jesus in their lives can also function as role models for new Christians.

*Observation.* Christians are called to closely observe Jesus and those who exemplify a Christlike life. We saw that the imitation of an 'absent' Jesus was not an insurmountable hurdle for early Christians because imitation was possible through other means than direct observation. John, for example, preserved Jesus' life and teachings in his gospel, so that his first and subsequent audiences could visualize (*ie* create a mental picture of) Jesus and study him. The new forms of imitation John introduces in his first letter, rooted in the example and teaching of Jesus, show that he expects Christians in the late first century to be able to imitate an absent Jesus. Paul employs a different strategy where he presents himself and other Christians as models worthy of imitation to his new converts. So Christians today can observe and study Jesus as seen in the biblical text or exemplified in the lives of commendable Christians. While the Bible articulates normative behaviour, Jesus' followers who can model authentic Christian living for younger Christians are also vital.

*Interpretation.* In studying Jesus or Christlike exemplars, Christians must discern what to imitate about them. Should they imitate (i) specific actions, (ii) the underlying intentions or attitudes or (iii) a general mindset of moral discernment? The imitation of Jesus must be guided by sound principles to prevent it from becoming an entirely subjective exercise. Take the WWJD movement which recognized the relevance of imitating Jesus but provided no guidelines on how. Others have a concept of imitation that is generic or imprecise, such as imitating Jesus' open acceptance of others,[24] or a 'broad, flexible approach to imitation.'[25] I propose that the *biblical text* and the *Spirit* should guide the imitation of Jesus. While Jesus is the model for Christian behaviour, this is true *only* to the extent that the biblical text indicates it because certain aspects or actions of Jesus cannot be imitated. To imitate Jesus appropriately we must determine the imitation language that the biblical authors use to avoid a subjective pick-and-mix approach. The Spirit aids the Christian in the interpretation of the biblical text and in determining what to imitate about Jesus. We will find that the imitation of Jesus centres on values such as humility, love, forgiveness, unity, self-giving and other-regard.

*Imitation.* Having studied and discerned what to imitate, the Christian must express this in appropriate ways that authentically convey the intention of the original example. At times, it is fitting to replicate a specific action of Jesus, always recognizing that this must include the original intent or attitude to avoid mindless cloning. At other times, the imitative act may differ from the original, while still expressing the intent or attitude of the original act. What is crucial is that the imitative act embodies the purpose and principle of the original and has a recognizable correspondence to the original act.

*Transformation.* As Christians seek to model their lives on Jesus, whether by picturing Jesus in the biblical text or by observing exemplary Christians, they gradually become more Christlike. We come full circle when we realize that imitating Jesus is not simply about personal growth but that the ultimate challenge is to become an example for others in their Christian journey.

A final word on the need for Christians to develop *moral reasoning* and a mindset of moral discernment as they embrace a lifestyle of imitating Jesus. We noted how early Christians applied moral reasoning: (i) John created new forms of imitation based on Jesus' example and teachings; (ii) Paul created a new mode of imitation where he could exhort his audiences to imitate him (or his surrogates); (iii) Christians in the second century developed a concept of martyrological imitation from New Testament teachings. Similarly today, Christians should use moral reasoning or discernment in this complex and creative process of imitating Jesus: (i) besides Jesus as the principal example for imitation, Christians must wisely select good role models; (ii) they are to study closely what they can imitate from these role models; (iii) they must determine creatively and carefully how to translate the role model's exemplary behaviour into a corresponding imitative act. In short, Christians should be (more) intentional about imitating Jesus in their discipleship.

## Questions for Discussion or Reflection

- What could help or hinder your efforts to determine which aspects or actions of Jesus are suitable for imitation when you study the biblical text? For example, should Christians seek to imitate Jesus' miracles (see John 14.12)?

- Who do you see as good role models in your environment, how do they exemplify Christ, and can you incorporate their example into your own life?
- In imitating others, how can we avoid creating a personality cult (see *eg* 1 Cor 3)?
- What can you do to be(come) an attractive role model of Christian living for others?

## Further Reading


C Bennema, *Imitation in Early Christianity: Mimesis and Religious-Ethical Formation* (Grand Rapids, MI: Eerdmans, 2025).

R A Burridge, *Imitating Jesus: An Inclusive Approach to New Testament Ethics* (Grand Rapids, MI: Eerdmans, 2007).

D B Capes, '*Imitatio Christi* and the Gospel Genre,' *Bulletin for Biblical Research* 13 (2003) pp 1–19.

A D Clarke, '"Be Imitators of Me": Paul's Model of Leadership,' *Tyndale Bulletin* 49 (1998) pp 329–360.

V A Copan, *Saint Paul as Spiritual Director: An Analysis of the Imitation of Paul with Implications and Applications to the Practice of Spiritual Direction* (Colorado Springs, CO: Paternoster, 2007).

J B Hood, *Imitating God in Christ: Recapturing a Biblical Pattern* (Downers Grove, IL: IVP Academic, 2013).

M Jensen, 'Imitating Paul, Imitating Christ: How Does Imitation Work as a Moral Concept?' *Churchman* 124 (2010) pp 17–36.

C R Moss, *The Other Christs: Imitating Jesus in Ancient Christian Ideologies of Martyrdom* (Oxford University Press, 2010).

# Notes

1 For a detailed study of imitation in the New Testament and Apostolic Fathers within the broader Graeco-Roman and Jewish world, see C Bennema, *Imitation in Early Christianity: Mimesis and Religious-Ethical Formation* (Grand Rapids, MI: Eerdmans, 2025).

2 New Testament: 1 Cor 4.16; 11.1; Eph 5.1; Phil 3.17; 1 Thess 1.6; 2.14; 2 Thess 3.7, 9; Heb 6.12; 13.7; 3 John 11. Apostolic Fathers: 1 Clem 17.1; Diogn 10.4-6 (4 times); Ign *Eph* 1.1; 10.2, 3; Ign *Magn* 10.1; Ign *Trall* 1.2; Ign. *Rom* 6.3; Ign *Phld* 7.2; Ign *Smyrn* 12.1; Pol *Phil* 1.1; 8.2; Mart Pol 1.2; 17.3; 19.1.

3 W P de Boer, *The Imitation of Paul: An Exegetical Study* (Kampen: Kok, 1962) pp 1-8.

4 *ibid*, pp 2, 15.

5 M C Nussbaum, 'Philosophy and Literature,' in D Sedley (ed), *The Cambridge Companion to Greek and Roman Philosophy* (Cambridge University Press, 2003) pp 216-217.

6 F Hörcher, 'Dramatic Mimesis and Civic Education in Aristotle, Cicero and Renaissance Humanism,' *Aisthesis* 10 (2017): 88-91.

7 E P J Corbett, 'The Theory and Practice of Imitation in Classical Rhetoric,' *College Composition and Communication* 22 (1971): 243.

8 English translations of Graeco-Roman excerpts are taken from the Loeb Classical Library.

9 See, for example, E W Davies, 'Walking in God's Ways: The Concept of *Imitatio Dei* in the Old Testament,' in E Ball (ed), *In Search of True Wisdom: Essays in Old Testament Interpretation in Honour of Ronald E Clements* (Sheffield: Sheffield Academic Press, 1999) pp 99-115; J Barton, *Ethics in Ancient Israel* (Oxford University Press, 2014) pp 263-272.

10 B Gerhardsson, *Memory and Manuscript: Oral Tradition and Written Transmission in Rabbinic Judaism and Early Christianity* (Grand Rapids, MI: Eerdmans, 1998) pp 182-187.

11 De Boer, *Imitation, op cit*, pp 146, 151.

12 V A Copan, *Saint Paul as Spiritual Director: An Analysis of the Imitation of Paul with Implications and Applications to the Practice of Spiritual Direction* (Colorado Springs, CO: Paternoster, 2007) p 140.

13 De Boer, *Imitation, op cit*, p 194.

14 De Boer, *Imitation, op cit*, p 62.

15 De Boer, *Imitation, op cit*, pp 214-216.

16 C A Barbarick, 'The Pattern and the Power: The Example of Christ in 1 Peter' (PhD diss, Baylor University, 2011) pp 92-94, 107-108.

**17** J Petitfils, *Mos Christianorum: The Roman Discourse of Exemplarity and the Jewish and Christian Language of Leadership* (Tübingen: Mohr Siebeck, 2016) pp 197–199.

**18** C R Moss, *The Other Christs: Imitating Jesus in Ancient Christian Ideologies of Martyrdom* (Oxford University Press, 2010) p 42.

**19** P Hartog, '*Imitatio Christi* and *Imitatio Dei*: High Christology and Ignatius of Antioch's Ethics,' *Perichoresis* 17 (2019): 14.

**20** See the entry 'μίμημα' in W Bauer *et al* (eds), *A Greek-English Lexicon of the New Testament and Other Early Christian Literature* (Chicago, IL: University of Chicago Press, 2000).

**21** P Hartog, *Polycarp and the New Testament: The Occasion, Rhetoric, Theme, and Unity of the Epistle to the Philippians and Its Allusions to New Testament Literature* (Tübingen: Mohr Siebeck, 2002) p 130.

**22** Moss, *Other Christs, op cit*, p 46.

**23** Moss, *Other Christs, op cit*, pp 47–48.

**24** R A Burridge, *Imitating Jesus: An Inclusive Approach to New Testament Ethics* (Grand Rapids, MI: Eerdmans, 2007) pp 77, 144–148, 183–184, 222–224, 280–283, 343–345.

**25** J B Hood, *Imitating God in Christ: Recapturing a Biblical Pattern* (Downers Grove, IL: IVP Academic, 2013) p 12 (but see also pp 74, 132–133).